Two Parts of Me

I am More Than My Body

Written by
Susan Nicholas, MD

Illustrated by
Basia Tran

Illustrated by Basia Tran
Cover Art & Design by Basia Tran

A Human Consciousness Consortium Hardcover
Atlanta, GA 30339
Website: www.SusanNicholas.org
Email: Books@SusanNicholas.org

ISBN (Hardcover) 978-1-7324336-1-8
ISBN (Paperback) 978-1-7324336-4-9
ISBN (e-book) 978-1-7324336-3-2

Library of Congress Control Number 2019903076

To my son Wolfie, the love of my life.
And to Hana, Tucker and Blake, I love you with all my heart.
S.N.

Did you know that there are two parts of you? The part of you that was born on a special day and given a name is your physical body. This is the part of you that the world sees.

WOLFIE

All bodies are
magnificent and unique
in their own ways.
The physical body has
weight and sensations.
It is what allows you
to have incredible
experiences on Earth.

There is another part of you that lives inside of your body. It is called your soul. The soul is pure energy and full of light.

Your soul can also be called your energy body. Your energy body gives you consciousness. Consciousness is what brings the physical part of you to life.

Your energy body has feelings like love and happiness.

Your energy body has other feelings like fear and sadness.

The energy body can look a lot like your physical body but does not have significant weight. It can move quickly and effortlessly when you are dreaming.

The energy body uses emotions to help you in making decisions in life. Your physical body interprets the feelings and emotions of the energy body.

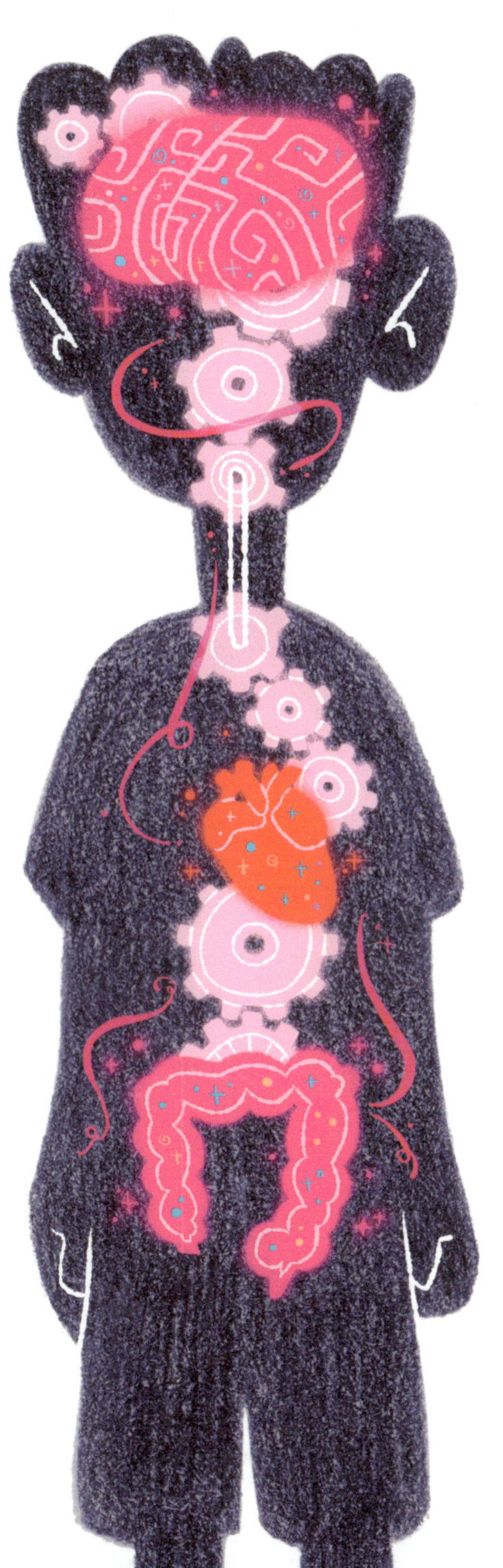

When you have a feeling in your heart or stomach, that is the pure energy part of you communicating with your physical body. It is important to listen when that happens.

Your energy body is your consciousness and wants to guide you.

When you have a strong feeling in your heart or other part of your body, ask your soul, "What are you trying to tell me?" Then listen for the answer.

Your energy body has great power. It is the part of you that dreams and the part of you that can soar. When you lay down in your bed to sleep, the energy body takes flight.

There will be times when you can remember your dreams.

And other times you will not. It's OK either way.

Your energy body is always attached to your physical body while you are alive on Earth. Your energy body cannot get lost when it flies. You are never alone, and the energy body always finds its way back to you.

When you are awake, your energy radiates outward, showing its light. This is your aura.

There are special people on Earth who can see your aura. Maybe you can see the auras of other people too!

There are two extraordinary parts that make up the whole you. The physical body and the energy body come together to form "one" you.

You are a wonderful and magnificent energy being having a human experience on Earth.

About the Author

Susan Nicholas, MD is the founder of the Human Consciousness Consortium, the publishing arm of Conscious Books. Susan is the author of *The Duality of Being: Perspectives from Multidimensional Travel* and *Two Parts of Me: I am More Than My Body*. *Two Parts of Me* is the first in a series of illustrated children's books on topics of intrigue and discourse from a conscious perspective. She is a Reiki energy healer, conscious life coach, and inspirational speaker on topics of consciousness for SusanNicholas.org.

Dr. Nicholas is a former clinical fellow in Cardiothoracic Surgery at Stanford University and General Surgery resident and research fellow at UCSF Medical Center.
Susan is a graduate of the University of Iowa College of Medicine and earned an Executive MBA from Emory University Goizueta Business School. After graduating from business school, Dr. Nicholas founded a healthcare company and worked as a healthcare equity investment analyst. Susan began her career as a pharmacokinetics chemist at a publicly traded pharmaceutical company. Susan is a French language and culture enthusiast, enjoys organic baking, running, swimming, and playing the violin. She lives in Atlanta, Georgia, with her son.

About the Illustrator

Basia Tran is a Polish-Vietnamese children's books and lifestyle illustrator, occasionally also working in music, animation, video games, and advertising. Her diverse work and interests are all connected by a common thread: her desire to tell stories that can make people laugh, teach them something new, or even bring them peace. In her free time, Basia is rock climbing, enjoying tea, and thinking about all there is to learn and explore in the universe – often all at the same time.

She is currently based in her hometown Kraków, Poland.

Author's Note:

Two Parts of Me: I am More Than My Body is the first in a series of Conscious Children's Books published by the Human Consciousness Consortium. This title came to me after my conscious awakening and during the time I was writing my first book for adults entitled *The Duality of Being: Perspectives From Multidimensional Travel*. At that time, I came to the realization that many of the emotional burdens we carry into adulthood originate in childhood.

I wondered if we could teach our children not only about their feelings but how to transform and release them, then perhaps there would be less suffering in the world. *Two Parts of Me* was written to remind children of their dual nature, that they are more than their physical body. It addresses the notion that the feelings emanating from our souls are present to guide us throughout life. The book is intended to allow children to remember who they truly are and to be empowered in this knowing.

Future *Conscious Children's Book* titles will include discussing death with children, gender identity, bullying, and learning or physical differences. All children's titles are non-fiction and written from a child's perspective with conscious awareness infused throughout the pages. Titles in this series are designed for children in kindergarten through 4th grade and ages 5-10 years.

Follow the Human Consciousness Consortium on Facebook.
Visit us at www.SusanNicholas.org and subscribe to receive updates on future releases.

In love and light,
Susan Nicholas, MD

www.ingramcontent.com/pod-product-compliance
Lightning Source LLC
LaVergne TN
LVHW070223110826
845147LV00003B/634

9781732433649